AF556076

LIFE LESSONS

'LIBERATE YOUR MIND'

India has produced some of the world's greatest religious leaders, sages, saints, philosophers, and spiritual thinkers. They were monks, nuns, and renunciates, nationalists and reformers. No one religion had a monopoly on them. They range from Mahavira and Buddha, who lived over 2,500 years ago, to medieval saints like Chishti, Avvaiyar, and Guru Nanak, to more recent philosophers and religious icons such as Vivekananda, Ramakrishna, Saint Teresa, and many others. The spiritual and philosophical heritage they left behind is India's gift to all Indians and the world.

In the 'Life Lessons' series we publish the essential teachings of some of India's best-known spiritual teachers, along with commentaries and biographical notes. Each book will be a handy companion to help the reader along the difficult pathways of life.

In the same series

'See Things As They Are': Life Lessons from the Buddha (ed.)Énanditha Krishna

'One Who Serves Becomes the Master': Life Lessons from Hazrat Nizamuddin (ed.) Bela Upadhyay

'Believe in Yourself': Life Lessons from Swami Vivekananda (ed.) Nanditha Krishna

'Looking Within': Life Lessons from Lal Ded (ed.) Shonaleeka Kaul

'Live and Let Others Live': Life Lessons from Mahavira (ed.) Nanditha Krishna

'The Light in All Is One': Life Lessons from Guru Nanak (ed.) Navkirat Sodhi

'You Are the Supreme Light': Life Lessons from Adi Shankara (ed.) Nanditha Krishna

'Be Present in Every Moment': Life Lessons from Moinuddin Chishti (ed.) Babli Parveen

'LIBERATE YOUR MIND'

~

LIFE LESSONS FROM

SRI RAMAKRISHNA

EDITED BY

Arpita Mitra

ALEPH BOOK COMPANY
An independent publishing firm
promoted by ***Rupa Publications India***

First published in India in 2023
by Aleph Book Company
7/16 Ansari Road, Daryaganj
New Delhi 110 002

ISBN: 978-93-93852-64-9

1 3 5 7 9 10 8 6 4 2

Printed in India.

SERIES INTRODUCTION

India has produced some of the world's greatest religious leaders, sages, saints, philosophers, and spiritual thinkers. They were monks, nuns, and renunciates, nationalists and reformers. No one religion had a monopoly on them. They range from Mahavira and Buddha, who lived over 2,500 years ago, to medieval saints like Chishti, Avvaiyar, and Guru Nanak, to more recent philosophers and religious icons such as Vivekananda, Ramakrishna, Saint Teresa, and many others. Each of them touched the lives of the people they lived among and the generations that followed. They inspired devotees and followers with their erudition and wisdom. The spiritual and philosophical heritage they left behind is India's gift to all Indians and the world.

Through the 'Life Lessons' series we will examine the teachings of some of India's best-known spiritual teachers. Each book will be a handy companion to help the reader along the difficult pathways of life.

Happiness and sorrow are unavoidable. The world is a place of trials and problems recur in every generation. Is suffering a necessary part of human life? How can one overcome suffering? Can hardship make a person stronger? What is happiness? Everybody wants to be happy, but how does one achieve this state? Does happiness come from vast riches and great achievements or does it come from the satisfaction of the soul? Is worldly success more important or is it fulfilment that one should seek?

These and similar questions vex every individual and have preoccupied the minds of philosophers and religious savants down the ages. The answers that these great souls found to life's conundrums occupy entire libraries worth of books and texts. This series is culled from their essential teachings and will present to readers some of the greatest truths to be found in India's spiritual heritage in a simple and accessible way. It is to be hoped that what you find here will prompt you to go deeper into the life and work of those who plumbed life's greatest mysteries.

Walking in the footsteps of these great men and women can take each of us to greater heights of knowledge, wisdom, and understanding. They can teach us how to find happiness and peace and the true meaning of well-being and success. Most of all, they can teach us how to value one another and cherish the holy gift of life.

'He (Sri Ramakrishna) was contented simply to live that great life and to leave it to others to find the explanation!'

—Swami Vivekananda

'The story of Ramakrishna Paramahamsa's life is a story of religion in practice. His life enables us to see God face to face.'

—Mahatma Gandhi

INTRODUCTION

Sri Ramakrishna Paramahamsa (1836–86) was an Indian saint who was born Gadadhar Chattopadhyay in a village in Bengal. In his adult life, he lived in the famous temple dedicated to Goddess Kali in Dakshineswar in the outskirts of colonial Calcutta (now Kolkata). The British, who ruled India for nearly two hundred years, had established Calcutta as the capital city of the British empire in India. The city was the fountainhead of all things Western introduced in India to consolidate imperial rule. Thus, nineteenth-century Calcutta was the mecca of materialism and home to the first generation of Indian intellectuals exposed to Western rationalism, who questioned the very existence of God. In such an age, Sri Ramakrishna demonstrated through his life that God not only exists but can also be *seen* if one's yearning for God is true and intense.

Ramakrishna's teachings, though presented mostly in the form of parables and allegories in the course of conversations, contain deep and sophisticated philosophical ideas that bridge the gap between tradition and modernity in the human experience of religion. He always insisted on the need to have a direct experience of God, as religion is not a matter of dogmas, doctrines, beliefs, and practices. He taught that while the supreme Godhead is transcendent, that is, independent of this phenomenal world, God is also immanent in this world. If one sees God only as an entity beyond the realm of the ever-changing, yet fails to perceive the divinity inherent in every being, one's God-realization is but incomplete. A devotee and child of Mother Kali, Ramakrishna preached to the world that all paths are equally true and capable of leading one to God. During his lifetime, he attracted a significant following, and is hailed by many today as a divine incarnation. His most famous disciple, Swami Vivekananda (1863–1902), established the twin organizations, Ramakrishna Math and Ramakrishna Mission, in his name, to preserve and propagate his teachings. These organizations now have branches all over the world.

In the north-western part of the Hooghly District in West Bengal lies the village of Kamarpukur. A much-travelled road went through Kamarpukur straight up to the sacred city of Puri in Odisha. The pilgrimage of Tarakeshwar Shiva was located not far away. Much earlier, the worship of Dharmathakur was quite prevalent in this village. Kamarpukur was like most other villages of Bengal—the lush, expansive, breezy agricultural land made life comfortable and peaceful, and the people were simple and devout by nature. In this sacred rural land, the fourth child of Khudiram Chattopadhyay and Chandramani Devi was born on 18 February 1836. They named him Gadadhar—he would come to be known to the world as Ramakrishna Paramahamsa.

Khudiram Chattopadhyay's ancestral village was Dere, where his family had lived for generations. Khudiram led a life of piety, austerity, and contentment. Ramananda Rai, the zamindar of the village, was notorious for his oppressive nature. Once, he filed a false case against someone and wanted Khudiram to give false witness. Knowing fully well what the consequences could be, Khudiram refused. In retaliation, the zamindar appropriated all his land and Khudiram had to leave the village without a single possession but with the responsibility of providing for his family comprising his wife and three children. This exceptional devotion to truth would be reflected in the life of his son Sri Ramakrishna as well.

The family was devoted to Rama and the three deities worshipped in the household were Raghuvir, Shitala, and Shiva. Chandramani Devi was a guileless, kind, and devout person. She had two sons and a daughter before Gadadhar's birth. The conception and birth of her last child was accompanied by several divine visions experienced by both parents. The child was named after Vishnu, the principal deity at Gaya,[1] where Khudiram had had the dream which indicated the imminent birth of an extraordinary child.

Khudiram passed away when Gadadhar was seven years old. A few years later, in 1849, Gadadhar's elder brother Ramkumar left for Calcutta for better prospects of livelihood; soon Gadadhar was brought to Calcutta. Around 1847, Rani Rashmoni, a wealthy widow belonging to the Kaivarta[2] caste, had purchased land in Dakshineswar, a village on the outskirts of Calcutta, for building a temple for her beloved Mother Kali. The temple was consecrated

---

[1]Gaya is famous for the Vishnupad temple.

[2]They were originally considered to be a low caste. It was very difficult to find a priest who would officiate the consecration ceremony of the temple built by a woman belonging to this caste.

in 1855, and Ramkumar Chattopadhyay was appointed priest of the Kali temple. In time, Gadadhar too became a priest at the temple. A few years after he had become a priest, Gadadhar was married to Saradamani Devi of the neighbouring village, Jayrambati. The bride and the groom were six and twenty-three years old respectively. Ramakrishna returned to Dakshineswar after the wedding, and the child bride stayed behind in the village.

Since boyhood, Gadadhar had had diverse spiritual experiences. His coming to Dakshineswar with Ramkumar intensified his spiritual longing and paved the way for a fuller awakening. He undertook intense sadhana[3] in diverse folds such as Tantra, Vaishnavism,

[3]Spiritual practice or austerities undertaken for attaining God-realization.

Vedanta, and Sufism and attained the best spiritual realizations available to humankind. It was in Dakshineswar that he got his new name 'Ramakrishna'. As a place of pilgrimage, Dakshineswar used to attract holy men and devotees from other parts of the country as well. In time, his fame spread far and wide. Many seekers and devotees from Calcutta began to flock to Dakshineswar to meet this unique saint. Ramakrishna too visited Calcutta on several occasions.

In the meantime, at the age of nineteen, Sarada Devi visited Dakshineswar for the first time. Thereafter, Sri Ramakrishna trained his consort in spiritual life, preparing her for the role she would take on after his death. In 1885, Sri Ramakrishna fell severely ill and was diagnosed with throat cancer. On 16 August

1886, at the age of fifty, he left his mortal body. He was survived by a band of dedicated young disciples led by Narendranath Dutta, a handful of householder devotees, and his consort, Sri Sarada Devi. The young disciples were ready to renounce the world and became itinerant monks. In due course, Narendranath became Swami Vivekananda and attained worldwide fame at the Parliament of Religions in Chicago in September 1893. In May 1897, he established the Ramakrishna Math and Ramakrishna Mission in Belur in the outskirts of Calcutta.

While the more dramatic incidents would occur in a different theatre in his adult life, Ramakrishna's life as a young village boy was by no means uninteresting. The incident around his upanayana (sacred thread ceremony) gives us a glimpse into his real personality. Dhani, the midwife who had delivered Gadadhar, had expressed a desire to become his bhiksha-mata[4] at his upanayana. Moved by her affection, the boy had heartily agreed to this request. A woman of the blacksmith caste becoming the bhiksha-mata of a Brahmin boy was unheard of in that orthodox family. When the time for his upanayana came, Gadadhar apprised his brother of his promise. Ramkumar refused to allow it, but Gadadhar was equally adamant. He argued that if he failed to keep his word, it would be a deviation from truth, and an untruthful person is, in the first place, not fit to wear the sacred thread. Finally, a family friend intervened and convinced Ramkumar. Gadadhar got his way.

Gadadhar was very gifted in creative

[4]The woman who offers the first bowl of rice as bhiksha or alms to the boy in the concluding ritual of upanayana.

pursuits like painting, making idols of gods and goddesses, and acting. But he was not interested in formal education. He would not do anything that was in contradiction to his principles in life. For instance, he could not learn mathematics because he was incapable of subtracting! God or the Ultimate Reality is one and indivisible—how can one subtract? When once reprimanded for his lack of interest in studies, Gadadhar replied that he was not interested in a 'chal-kala-bandha bidya'[5] (bread-winning education) and would rather pursue the goal of real knowledge.

It was quite difficult to persuade Gadadhar to take up employment as the temple priest at

[5]The expression literally means knowledge that helps one tie up rice and bananas in a cloth—the allusion is to the common practice of priests of tying up rice, fruits, vegetables, and other food items that they receive as dakshina (fees for priestly service) in a piece of cloth at the households where they perform religious ceremonies.

Dakshineswar. All he wanted was to be in the service of God and nobody else. A temple priest draws salary from the owners of the temple after all. As a matter of fact, he never collected his salary by signing in the accounts book. Just as soil cannot help a seeker attain God, similarly, money is just as useless in the pursuit of God. Thinking this, he once took some soil and coins and dropped them into the Ganga uttering 'Taka mati, mati taka' (money is soil, soil is money). Gradually he reached a state wherein he could touch neither money nor any metal object—contact with these objects caused a painful sensation in his hands. He was free from the desire for wealth, but that did not mean he was careless about spending. Later he would advise his disciples to be mindful of wastage and to always spend judiciously. He also told them that it was the duty of householders to practise generous charity.

When Ramkumar entered service at the temple at Dakshineswar, Ramakrishna was around nineteen years old. For the next twelve years, Ramakrishna would undertake different kinds of sadhana to realize God. Ramkumar passed away within a year of the consecration of the temple and Ramakrishna plunged even deeper into sadhana with the intense desire to *see* his Divine Mother. He spent his days completely absorbed in her contemplation. After the daily worship, he would sit in front of the divine image and sing devotional songs to her, gradually losing himself in ecstatic love for the Mother. His yearning grew so much that he prayed and wept all day and night. Gradually, it became so unbearable that one day he rushed to take Kali's sword and put an end to his futile life. It was then that he received her darshan (vision of the Divine) and fell down. Room, door, temple, everything disappeared and all he saw was an endless infinite ocean of light that rapidly engulfed him and he lost all consciousness of the outer world. When he finally emerged out of this state, his first utterance was 'Mother'.

The first vision of the Divine Mother intensified his desire to see her again and again. This desire often translated into behaving in a way that seemed insane to the people around him. He would roll on the floor and cry desperately. Often in such circumstances, he passed into meditative states, and was eventually blessed by the vision of the Mother, smiling, speaking to him, assuring and instructing him. On several occasions, he actually saw this Divine

Consciousness residing in and emanating from the idol of Mother Kali (Bhavatarini) in the shrine. Naturally, the one who spent much time in such states of spiritual ecstasy, gradually became incapable of executing his practical duties at the temple. His worship assumed a unique and unprecedented form which was beyond the comprehension of common people. His relatives now tried to get him treated for what they thought was some kind of malady. His colleagues complained to the temple authorities. But Rani Rashmoni and her son-in-law Mathur Babu, after seeing the curious worship of the mad priest, became convinced that he was an exceptionally pure soul, blessed with true spiritual vision.

The sole guiding force during this initial period of his sadhana leading up to the vision of the Divine Mother was his single-minded devotion and soulful yearning for the Divine. It was such an intense yearning that it made the entire material world around him appear non-existent. During this period, he also worshipped his family deity Raghuvir in the dasya bhava[6] by cultivating in himself the qualities of Hanuman. He also had a unique spiritual vision—he saw the magnificent Sita in front of him; she eventually entered his body.

All these incidents transpired during the first four years of his stay at Dakshineswar. Thereafter, he was married off by his family, who

[6]There are five personal attitudes one can take towards the Divine: shanta, dasya, sakhya, vatsalya, and madhura. The first one is the attitude that the sages had towards Rama. Dasya is the attitude of being a servant of God (Hanuman towards Rama, for instance), and sakhya that of friendship with God (Arjuna towards Krishna). In vatsalya, one treats God as one's child (Yashoda towards Krishna), and in madhura, one becomes a lover of God (Radha and Krishna).

thought that the marriage might help normalize the mad Gadadhar. But Ramakrishna's was not an illness that it would be cured! His spiritual longing only increased over time. Rani Rashmoni passed away in February 1861. Shortly thereafter, an important guest arrived at Dakshineswar. Yogeshwari, popularly known as Bhairavi Brahmani, was an accomplished Tantra practitioner and preceptor. She was elated to meet Ramakrishna, who sat before her like a child and recounted his spiritual experiences. Bhairavi assured him that his mental states were not fits of insanity but high spiritual states, which were experienced by extraordinary souls like Radha, the divine consort of Krishna, and Chaitanya, the saint of medieval Bengal believed to be an incarnation of Krishna. For the next two years, with Bhairavi Brahmani as his Tantra guru, Ramakrishna performed all the sixty-four practices prescribed in Tantra and attained the spiritual fruits thereof. But his Tantra sadhana was different from the usual in that he could never partake of karan[7] nor cultivate virbhava[8] towards women. Ramakrishna's attitude of looking upon women as mother remained intact all through his Tantra sadhana. During this period, he also had the vision of the Divine Mother in different forms. One important fruit of Tantra sadhana is that it removes from the mind the so-called difference between the pure and the impure and brings the devotee to truly seeing oneness.

Ramakrishna undertook sadhana as per the

[7]Sanctified liquor used in Tantra sadhana.
[8]One of the attitudes prescribed in Tantra in which the aspirant, who is a man, regards himself as purusha and woman as prakriti and tries to please her accordingly.

Vaishnava path once again. He now sought to practise the two chief sadhana paths within Vaishnavism—vatsalya bhava and madhura bhava, both of which required the aspirant to mentally be a woman. The requisite mental attitude was present in him as he had already started to look upon himself as a sakhi (female friend) and dasi (female servant) of the Divine Mother. Sometime in 1863–64, a sadhu named Jatadhari arrived at Dakshineswar, with his Ramlala—an image of the child form of Rama. Ramakrishna had earlier received spiritual initiation with the sacred name of Rama; now, he received initiation with the name of Gopal, the child-form of Krishna, from Jatadhari and relished the new feeling of vatsalya bhava towards Ramlala. Soon he had the divine vision of child Rama, and also realized the all-pervasive immanence of Rama—'Jo Ram Dasarath ka beta, wohi Ram ghat-ghat me leta!'[9] It was time for Jatadhari to leave, but his Ramlala expressed the desire to stay with Ramakrishna. So, handing over Ramlala, Jatadhari left Dakshineswar.

Madhura bhava is the highest form of love for the Divine. It requires the absolute superimposition of the attitude of a woman. During this sadhana, Ramakrishna dressed like a woman, and had such immaculate womanly mannerisms that no one could tell who he was. Ramakrishna first spent his days in meditation, meditating on Sri Radha, whose vision he was soon blessed with. Since then, he started identifying with her. With an intense yearning for Krishna such as Radha's, even his body

---

[9]That Rama who is the son of Dasarath is also the Rama who is the content of every form.

underwent a transformation. This sadhana culminated in the blissful vision of Sri Krishna, who eventually merged into Ramakrishna's own person.

Two or three months later, Srimat Tota Puri, a well-known sadhu of Adi Sankara's monastic order, arrived in Dakshineswar. He was surprised to see an aspirant like Ramakrishna and offered to instruct him in Advaita Vedanta. Ramakrishna received sannyasa (monastic vow) from Tota Puri and experienced nirvikalpa samadhi[10]—the last word in Advaita sadhana—in just three days. And he remained in that state continuously for three days till it was broken by Tota Puri

[10]Samadhi is the spiritual state, usually attained through meditation, in which a person experiences the Divine. Nirvikalpa samadhi is that kind of samadhi in which the triple distinction between knower, act of knowing, and object known is erased, that is, the I-consciousness of the one in meditation merges completely into the formless, attributeless, absolute Divine.

himself. Thereafter, Ramakrishna remained in that high spiritual mood for nearly six months. His spiritual journey, however, did not end here. He also took initiation from the Sufi Govind Rai and did sadhana according to Islamic teachings. He also had a vision of Jesus Christ, who, like the others, merged into Ramakrishna's own body. Through direct spiritual experiences, he realized that all paths equally lead to God.

Sri Ramakrishna's devotees in Calcutta included established personalities like Keshab Chandra Sen[11] (1838–1884), Girish Chandra Ghosh[12] (1844–1912), Mahendralal Sircar[13]

---

[11]Founder of Brahmo Samaj of India (1866) and later of Nava Vidhan or New Dispensation (1881).

[12]Actor and prolific playwright responsible for the golden age of Bengali proscenium theatre in the nineteenth century.

[13]Physician and founder of the Indian Association for the Cultivation of Science (1876).

(1833–1904), Mahendranath Gupta[14] (1854–1932), and others. The young disciples, most of whom later became monks, included sons of educated middle-class families, with the single exception of Latu (later Swami Adbhutananda), a servant of Ramakrishna's devotee, Ram Chandra Datta. It is of interest here to recount one of the early conversations between Ramakrishna and Narendranath, the future Vivekananda. Naren was around eighteen years old and was seeking God. 'Have you seen God?' was the question he put to the Brahmo Samaj leaders and to others, but did not find a satisfactory answer till he asked Ramakrishna the same question at their first meeting.

[14]Teacher who taught at the Metropolitan Institution (now Vidyasagar College) founded by Iswar Chandra Vidyasagar. Mahendranath Gupta is known to the world as 'M', the recorder of Ramakrishna's teachings in *Sri Sri Ramakrishna Kathamrita*.

Ramakrishna's reply was startling: 'Yes, I have seen God. Just as I see you. In fact, more clearly. God can be seen. But, my child, who wants to see God? People shed tons of tears for wife, children, and wealth; but who weeps for a vision of God?' He then told Naren that he too could see God if he followed the prescribed methods. It was the authenticity in this promise of direct perception of God that appealed to the intensely rational Narendranath. He was equally moved by the all-encompassing love of the saint.

Sri Ramakrishna was the ideal student, imbibing the best learning from the best teachers. He was also the ideal teacher who could understand the difference in the temperaments and requirements of individual disciples. Once he admonished his disciple Jogin (later Swami Yogananda) for not protesting against a slander against his guru Ramakrishna, as the inaction was due to Jogin's mental weakness. On the other hand, once Niranjan (later Swami Niranjanananda) lost his temper when he heard people defame Sri Ramakrishna. When he heard about the incident later, Ramakrishna told Niranjan to learn to control his anger.

Ramakrishna could also differentiate between the life-contexts of different devotees. Hence, he gave different instructions to his householder devotees and to those who would renounce the world. That is not to say that there can be any compromise in spiritual life. Such a life demands renunciation—only the outer form varies in the case of the householder, the inner life has to evince the same devotion, renunciation, and longing for God that is asked of a sannyasin. Ramakrishna himself was the model before his devotees; he was the ideal householder as well as the ideal sannyasin. A person like him, who could hardly look after himself, took every care to ensure the well-being of his mother and wife. On the other hand, his life was an embodiment of the most spontaneous and perfect renunciation; he demonstrated that renunciation is possible under all circumstances. It is believed that the swan, called hamsa in India, has a unique capacity: if one mixes milk and water, the swan, which can differentiate between the two, will drink the milk and leave behind the water. Thus, a Paramahamsa (literally the 'supreme swan') is a holy person who is capable of differentiating between the ephemeral and the eternal, accepting only that which is unchanging, that is, God, and rejecting the transitory. A Paramahamsa usually does this in a spontaneous act of renunciation while still living in the body. Great saints are thus often called Paramahamsas. It is not known definitively when and how Ramakrishna acquired this epithet, but it was during his Dakshineswar days that some devotees started referring to him as Paramahamsadev.

Ramakrishna was also an ideal jnani and an ideal bhakta. A jnani is a person who follows the jnana marga, that is, the path that usually emphasizes the attributeless (nirguna) and formless (nirakara) nature of God. For the jnani, in the ultimate analysis, God is transcendent and transpersonal, and the world with manifold names and forms (namarupa) is merely God's play (lila). A bhakta is a person who enjoys the personhood of God. A bhakta joins himself/herself in a personal relationship with God who has form and attributes. Both the jnani and the bhakta know God to be the Ultimate Reality, but their modes of spiritual practice are different. In this intensely materialistic age, Ramakrishna demonstrated that God can be attained by simple, unconditional devotion of the heart alone. This is bhakti marga or the path of devotion. His own bhakti was so unconditional that he never even asked his Divine Mother to cure his cancer. The same Ramakrishna attained non-dual consciousness with great ease and was firmly established in the spiritual experience of Advaita. This is the path shown by jnana marga. Even among Ramakrishna's devotees, one can observe a marked variation of temperaments—some liked God with form, some without form, and Ramakrishna could cater to all their diverse spiritual needs. This ability to address people from different standpoints made Sri Ramakrishna a fit teacher for people with different kinds of minds, spiritual aptitudes, and life circumstances.

Ramakrishna's teachings can be divided into different categories. Some teachings reflected general and universal principles. Other teachings were contextual and based on the requirement of the recipient. Again, certain teachings were given in deep meditative moods. For example, Ramakrishna's teaching of Shiva jnane jiva seva or serving God in man was given in the wake of his mind descending to this plane of existence from a state of samadhi. He also taught through action. For instance, he once banished one of his devotees just because the latter had the habit of bad-mouthing fellow devotees. At the same time, he gave absolute freedom to his devotees.

Naren would argue with him. Girish Ghosh would come to him in the middle of the night, absolutely drunk. Ramakrishna would receive him with utmost love and care.

Ramakrishna's relationship with women is worth discussing. He was a favourite of the village women; they would spend hours talking to the young boy, and listening to him sing devotional songs. Motherhood was a central theme in his life. He was very close to his own mother, whom he served diligently especially after the death of his father. Even later in life, he would tell his devotees to perform their duties towards their widowed mothers. His relationship with his wife was unique. It was filled with sweetness, mutual care, and deep respect. He observed all the duties towards his wife from instructing her in spiritual life to taking care of her when she was unwell. He also got a pair of golden bangles made for her as his mother had promised to the child bride. Furthermore, he got a nominal endowment done in her name so that after his death she would get a modest monthly pension for her upkeep. These were done with the money from his salary, which he never claimed for himself but which the temple authorities kept aside for his expenditure. Sarada Devi later remarked that Sri Ramakrishna had never hurt her even with a flower. But he had renounced marriage inwardly. When Ramakrishna had taken the vow of sannyasa with Tota Puri as his guru, the latter had told him that only that man, who can look upon both man and woman as the same sexless atman (soul), has truly realized Brahman. Sarada Devi was a collaborator in his spiritual life. The marriage was never consummated. Ramakrishna did not sire children, but he predicted that his wife would become the mother of hundreds and thousands in times to come. In order to awaken the latent divinity within her, he worshipped her as Shodashi Tripurasundari[15] on the night of Phalaharini Kali Puja[16] in 1872.

Ramakrishna had many women disciples. Notable among them were the daring ascetic Gauri Ma, and women devotees of high spiritual merit like Jogen Ma, Golap Ma, Gopaler Ma, and Lakshmi Didi. Gauri Ma had received direct instruction from Ramakrishna to work for the welfare of Indian women and rescue

---

[15]One among the ten Mahavidyas, a highly benevolent form of the Divine Mother.

[16]This particular Kali puja is performed on the new moon night of the lunar month of Jyestha (usually May–June of the Gregorian calendar).

them from their plight. Both Sri Ramakrishna and Sri Sarada Devi were the refuge of some well-known 'public women', who were actresses in the newly emerging proscenium theatre in nineteenth-century Calcutta. The great thespian Nati Binodini[17] was blessed by Sri Ramakrishna, who passed into a meditative state after watching her portrayal of Sri Chaitanya. Binodini records in her autobiography[18] how his grace and compassion offered a haven in her life otherwise full of personal suffering and social chastisement. Ramakrishna was thus the refuge of those who were despised by society. He could see their goodness and devotion. In the words of Vivekananda, Ramakrishna was

[17]Born as Binodini Dasi (1863–1941) into a family of sex workers, she was brought to the world of theatre by Girish Chandra Ghosh and became its leading light in no time.
[18]Binodini, *Amar Katha*, 1913.

'the saviour of women, saviour of the masses, saviour of all, high and low'. He lived to root out all differences—differences between 'man and woman, between the rich and the poor, the literate and illiterate, Brahmins and Chandalas'. He heralded a new age—an age where the masses and women would live with dignity and self-assurance.

Sri Ramakrishna was mad after God, but he was not indifferent to the miseries of the world. His compassion knew no bounds. Be it the sorrow of the rich or the poor, he stood equally by everybody's side. When his devotee Manimohan Mallick lost his young son and came to Ramakrishna, the latter was so overwhelmed with grief that it was as if his own son had died. Once when Ramakrishna saw the abject condition of the subjects of Rani

Rashmoni owing to the failure of crops, he insisted that their tax for that year be written off and they be served food and given new clothes. On another occasion, when on a pilgrimage to Baidyanathdham in Deoghar, he was moved by the condition of the tribal people of the region. He refused to leave that place until his patron, Mathur Babu, agreed to offer them oil and arrange for their bath, give them new clothes, and feed them a full meal. In Dakshineswar, he himself served the sweeper of the temple and other poor devotees. One time he was happy to see that his disciple Shashi (later Swami Ramakrishnananda) had bought a small knife from a fair, as poor people made different things and brought them to the fair in the hope of earning something. His compassion sprang from truly seeing the divine in one and all. Thus it was that one day in 1884 Ramakrishna, while descending from a state of samadhi, exclaimed that it was blasphemy to think of having daya or compassion for living beings, we are to instead practise Shiva jnane jiva seva, that is, service of man knowing him to be an embodiment of God.

He taught that to know the world as manifold is ignorance; to know it as one Divine Reality is knowledge. 'I' and 'mine' indicate limited subjectivity and a sense of possession, and are as such, expressions of ignorance; to know that everything belongs to God is knowledge. God is the only Reality; everything else in this world is impermanent. The goal of human life is God-realization. God can be seen, realized in this life, in this world itself. So long as one has genuine longing, one will find God. One who abides in truth will find God. There can be no spiritual advancement without renunciation; the householder is to renounce mentally, while the monk is to renounce both inwardly and outwardly. God can be reached through different paths, and all religions of the world are, in this sense, true. God is both with attributes (saguna) and without attributes (nirguna), with form (sakara) and without form (nirakara). The human soul is nothing but the immortal atman. Despite having tasted the formless Divine Absolute, Ramakrishna looked upon God as the Divine Mother, and upheld the idea of the Motherhood of God as especially suitable for this age. He looked upon all women as the embodiment of the Divine Mother. He himself was motherly, his young disciples recorded how he looked after them just as a mother would.

These are some of Ramakrishna

Paramahamsa's principal teachings which he demonstrated through his life. He could never utter the words 'I' and 'mine'. He was so bereft of body-consciousness that even when he was in physical pain during his illness, he continued to pass into blissful meditative states. He was grounded in the spiritual experience of advaita, and yet could travel seamlessly back to this world and see it as God immanent. He used to say—do we see God only in meditation, with our eyes closed? Can we not see Him all around with open eyes? Such a person is bound to be empathetic. Once when somebody walked over the young grass cover in the temple premises, Ramakrishna felt the pain for hours. He would dive into the deep waters of the inner realm every now and then but was equally capable of great humour and child-like merriment. He was full of child-like simplicity, but was also intensely practical and rational. Ramakrishna could make the most profound philosophical statements and yet present them in simple parables. He lived the great life and showed us that God can be realized in all circumstances.

NOTES ON THE TRANSLATION

All linguistic translation is essentially cultural translation. The difficulty of cultural translation presents itself even more powerfully in the case of aphorisms by someone like Sri Ramakrishna, who used Bengali idioms and rustic motifs liberally and spoke in a language that was not only colloquial but also his own. In light of these constraints, it is hoped that the shortcomings of the translation presented here will be excused.

Ramakrishna's aphorisms are mostly in the form of conversations. They are also highly contextual—the slant of his teachings was different depending on whether he was addressing a householder or a person who would renounce everything in the search for God. It would therefore not be surprising to come across seemingly contrary statements once in a while, as they were made in different contexts.

Ramakrishna addressed God with various names—Sacchidananda,[19] Rama, Mother, Bhagavan, Isvara, Hari, and so on (incidentally, his most common mode of address was 'sacchidananda'). Most of these have been translated as 'God' unless it was felt that it should be otherwise in that particular context. The third person pronoun in Bengali does not indicate the gender of the person in question. Hence, when Ramakrishna uses the third person pronoun for God, he does not specify whether he is referring to God's male or female form or

[19]Pure consciousness, God.

to the attributeless Brahman.[20] This third person pronoun for God has been mostly translated here as the masculine pronoun in English with the first letter in upper case—He, Him, His, unless it is clear from the context that Ramakrishna is referring to the Divine Mother. Though Brahman or Sacchidananda are not gendered entities, the masculine personal pronoun has been used to designate them—the use of 'it' has been avoided as Brahman is not an inanimate object.

In Bengali, nouns and pronouns for human beings also do not indicate the gender. Liberty has been taken to translate these mostly as 'man' or 'he'. This has been done purely from the point of view of ease of language, without any intention of perpetuating gender bias.

[20]The great cosmic being; according to the Upanishads, this is the one and only reality.

LIFE LESSONS

Do not speak ill of anyone,
not even of the insect.
There is no other quality that equals forbearance. The one who endures is the one who outlasts.

If a stone lies under water even for thousands of years, water does not enter it; but soil immediately absorbs water and becomes mud. Those who have faith and devotion do not get disappointed even in the midst of a thousand troubles; however, those who do not have faith get disturbed by the slightest trouble.

When one has to live in this world, one has to display a little bit of tamoguna[21] to save oneself from evil persons. But just because evil persons would harm one, one should not in turn harm them.

God is present in all beings. But one can associate only with good people; the company of bad people is to be avoided. God is present even in the tiger; that doesn't mean one is to embrace the tiger!

[21]Hindus believe that the universe is the combination of three gunas or qualities: sattva, rajas, tamas. Sattva symbolizes light, transparency, calmness, and equilibrium, in other words, all good and godly qualities. Rajas symbolizes passion, activity, anger, ego, and so on. Tamas represents darkness, lethargy, ignorance, in other words, certain evil tendencies. All three are present in everyone in varying degrees; some manifest more of sattvaguna, while others manifest more of rajoguna or tamoguna.

WORK

Work is not the goal of life; it is just the beginning of the story. Work without attachment is a path for God-realization, not the goal.

Work done without the expectation of return leads to the purification of the mind, devotion arises in the pure mind, and God can be attained by such devotion.

The kind of work that you are doing is good. If you can do it abjuring the idea that 'I am the doer' and without wanting to enjoy the fruits thereof, then it is very good. While working in such unattached manner, one develops devotion and love for God. One attains God doing work in such manner.

Everybody is engaged in work in some form or the other. Recounting the glories of God—that is also work. The contemplation of soham,[22] 'I am that'—that is also action. Breathing—that is also an activity. It is not possible to give up work altogether. Therefore, work! But offer the fruits of your work to God.

When a drunkard has drunk too much, he is no longer in his senses. If one drinks a little, one can still continue to work. The more you advance towards God, the less responsibility of work will befall you.

[22]'I am that', the advaitic position of non-duality.

WELFARE OF THE WORLD

Compassion! Helping others! What is our capacity that we may help others? Compassion belongs to God. How can human beings show compassion? Charity happens only by the will of God.

Welfare of others—that is possible only for God—the one who has created the sun and the moon, father and mother, fruits and grains for the welfare of all beings! The love that you see in parents is His love; He has endowed them with love for the protection of all beings. The compassion that you see in the compassionate person, is His compassion, which He has provided for the protection of the meek and the helpless. Whether you show compassion or not, He will work through some means or the other. His work will not be disrupted.

If a householder practises charity without any expectation of return, in the spirit of non-attachment, he ends up doing good to himself. It is not an act of 'helping' others. It is service rendered to God who resides in all beings.

WEALTH

Many people consider money to be like the blood in their body. But if one cares too much for money, one is eventually not able to enjoy it.

Those who make righteous use of money, such as in service to God, service rendered to monks and devotees, and charity, money serves some purpose only for them.

What can money get you? Food, clothing, a roof above your head—that's all. Money cannot help you attain God. That is why earning money cannot be the purpose of life.

When one has too much wealth, one forgets God. That is the nature of wealth.

Someone: Sir, can we strive to make more money?

Sri Ramakrishna: If it is for the sake of serving God, you can. But by fair means. Earning money is not the objective; the purpose is to serve God. If that money can help you serve God, there is no harm in it.

Sadhus[23] will depend completely on God. They are not supposed to save for the future. But that is not applicable for householders. Householders need money to look after their families. They need to have savings. The bird and the sannyasin[24] are the only ones who

[23]Usually means holy men who have taken the vow of monasticism.
[24]One who has taken the vow of monasticism.

ought not save for the future. But even the bird has to stock food when it has a birdling.

It is true that one needs money for sustenance, but do not think about that too much. Those who have surrendered their mind and heart to God, those who are God's devotees, who have taken refuge in Him—they do not think much about money. They receive as much money as they need to spend. Money comes from one end, and is expended at another end.

EGO

'I' and 'mine' do not let us know the truth.

It is very difficult to be free from the sense of the ego. If you grate onion and garlic and keep it in a bowl, the bowl will smell of onion and garlic no matter how much you rinse it. Just like that, a trace of ego always remains.

Only a handful of people experience samadhi[25] in a way that their ego disappears, but mostly it does not disappear completely.

---

[25]An exalted state of consciousness, where through meditation, thought-waves of the mind recede or subside, body consciousness disappears, one's body and mind become absolutely still, and one has a vision of the Divine.

No matter how much you reason, the ego comes back. Uproot an asvattha[26] tree today, and it will grow back tomorrow morning! If the 'I' will not go away completely, then let it remain as the 'I' of the 'servant of God'. 'Oh Lord! You are the master, and I am thy servant'—let it remain with this attitude. 'I am God's servant', 'I am God's devotee'—there is no harm in such 'I'.

The 'I' that makes us worldly, attached to objects of desire, that 'I' is bad. The difference between jiva[27] and atman[28] is caused by this 'I'. When you place a stick on the surface of water, it seems to divide the

---

[26]Peepul

[27]Ordinary human being; the body-mind complex in human beings.

[28]Literally means 'self'; the true self of human beings, the microcosmic counterpart of the macrocosmic Brahman; according to the non-dualists, it is identical with Brahman.

water into two. But in reality, the water is one; it appears as two because of the stick. The ego is the stick. Take out the stick, and you have undivided water.

I am asking you to give up the unripe 'I'—the 'I' that makes one attached to objects of desire. But I am not asking you to give up the mature 'I'...'I am God's servant, I am His child'—this is the mature 'I'.

One cannot attain God if one has the slightest trace of egotism.

DESIRE

One does not attain God if one has even the slightest trace of desire. Just like a thread that has even a tiny lump does not pass through the eye of a needle. When the mind becomes pure by being free from desire, it is only then that one attains Sacchidananda.

What is a mind free from desire like? It is like a dry matchstick—you rub it once and it will catch fire immediately. But when you try to light a wet match, you may rub it again and again till it breaks, but it will not burn. Similarly, when you give spiritual instruction to a simple, truthful, and pure-minded person, he immediately develops love for God. On the other hand, no matter how many times you instruct worldly people, it is to no avail.

The desire for bhakti[29] is not counted as desire.

---

[29]Loving devotion to God.

SIN

The person who says 'I am bound', 'I am bound' all the time, bound he becomes. The one who repeats day and night 'I am a sinner', 'I am a sinner', becomes a sinner.

One has to have this kind of faith in God's name—'What! I have taken God's name, can I still be a sinner? Do I have any sin any longer? What bondage do I have?'

When one dies while contemplating God, sin cannot touch that person any more.

Someone: Duryodhana had said 'O Krishna, you are the one who resides in my heart and makes me do as I do.'

Sri Ramakrishna: Yes, it is true that God is making us do everything, He is the doer and human beings are like instruments. But it is equally true that actions have consequences. If you eat chilies, you will have a burning sensation in your stomach. God Himself has warned you that if you eat chilies, you will have a burning sensation. If you commit sin, you have to suffer for it.

The one who has realized God is incapable of committing any sin. An expert dancer does not take a step out of rhythm. One who has practised music will always sing in tune.

PEACE

The more you advance towards God, the greater peace you experience. Peace, peace, peace, great peace. The nearer you get to the Ganges, the cooler you feel. Take a dip and you will feel even more peaceful.

DOUBT & FAITH

All doubts are quelled when one has the vision of the atman.

One cannot attain God unless one has a childlike faith.

Why say 'blind faith'? Faith itself is blind! Can faith have eyes? Either just say faith, or say knowledge.

TRUTH

One who is holding on to truth is lying in the lap of God.

Those who are engaged in worldly activities—even they should abide by truth. Truthfulness is the great austerity.

Abide in truth, you'll have God-realization.

MAYA[30]

One's ego is verily maya. This ego-sense has covered everything. 'All woes will come to an end when the "I" will die.'[31] If, by the grace of God, one develops the attitude 'I am not the doer', then one becomes jivanmukta.[32]

This maya or ego is like a cloud. One cannot see the Sun because of the presence of a little cloud—but the Sun can be seen when the cloud has disappeared. Similarly, if by

[30]Maya has been described variously: it means the empirical, phenomenal world; the veil of ignorance that covers truth; the power of God.

[31]A Bengali saying.

[32]One who continues to be in the body even after liberation or one who has attained liberation even while being in the body.

the grace of one's guru, one's ego-sense disappears, then one can see God.

It is on account of maya that sat[33] appears as asat,[34] and asat as sat. Sat means that which is eternal—parabrahman;
asat is the ephemeral world.

Do you know what maya is? It is attachment and love for one's own relatives—father, mother, brother, sister, wife, son, nephew, niece, and so on. And daya[35] means knowing that my Hari resides in all and thus loving all equally.

Do you know what is the nature of maya? Think of a pond covered with moss. You

---

[33]Existent, indestructible, eternal, true.
[34]Non-existent, that is, subject to change and destruction, ephemeral, false.
[35]Compassion.

move aside the moss and the moss recedes. But after some time, it comes back and covers the pond. Similarly, so long as you are discerning, or keeping holy company, you feel you are free from attachment. After some time, the desire for worldly objects comes back and enwraps you.

Maya takes flight once you recognize her.

WHO AM I?

Man can know God only when he knows himself. 'Who am I?'—when you try to reflect on this carefully, you'll see that there is in fact nothing called 'I'. Hands, feet, blood, flesh, and so on—which one of these is 'I'? When you peel an onion layer after layer, you will only get the skin, and no substance. Similarly, when you reason, you will see that there is no 'I'! What remains is the atman—consciousness. When the 'I'-ness of the 'I' disappears, God appears before us.

Who am I? When you try to know this, you end up finding God. Am I flesh, or bones, or blood, or marrow—or mind, or intelligence?

When you reason, you find that you are none of these. 'Neti', 'neti'.[36] It is not possible to get hold of the atman. It is without qualities, and without attributes.

Human beings are of the nature of sacchidananda. But maya or ego-sense has created so many finite attributes for them that they have forgotten their true selves.

Human beings are like pillows. The outer cloth is different for each—some are red, some are black, but the same cotton is to be found inside every pillow. So it is with human beings. Some are good-looking, some are not,

[36]'Not this', 'not this'. In Vedanta, if we want to proceed towards self-knowledge, we have to start with negation—what we are not; in order to know the ultimate reality Brahman, we first have to know what it is not.

some are of good character, some are not,
but the same God resides within all.

The pure atman is without any attachment. One cannot see the pure atman. When salt is mixed with water, one cannot see the salt.... This pure atman is our real nature.

GOD AND US

God-realization is the goal of human life.

His life is futile, who, having attained this difficult-to-attain human body does not make efforts to attain Sacchidananda.

You see, so long as one has the desire for worldly enjoyment, one's heart does not yearn for God. The child remains busy with playthings. Give him a candy, he'll taste it. When he doesn't want to play any more, and he doesn't like candies either, then he says, 'Take me to my mother'. He doesn't want candies any more. Even if a stranger offers to take him to his mother, he eagerly accompanies him.

KNOWLEDGE AND IGNORANCE

He [God] is the master and all this creation belongs to Him—this is knowledge. And 'I am the master', 'I am the guru', 'I am the father'—all this is ignorance. And this house, family, wealth, servants belong to me—this is ignorance.

'I' and 'mine'—these two represent ignorance.

What is knowledge? And who am I? God alone is the doer and nobody else is—this is knowledge. I am not the doer, but merely an instrument in God's hands.

What is knowledge and what is ignorance? So long as you feel that God is far away, out there somewhere, it is ignorance. When you feel He is near at hand, it is knowledge.

Both knowledge and ignorance are states of the mind. A human being is bound or free in the mind itself, a saint or sinner in the mind. If a person can practise continuous remembrance of God in the mind, no other form of sadhana is required.

When one has right knowledge, one sees everything as full of divine consciousness.

What is knowledge? Knowledge is to know one's real nature, that is pure atman, and to contemplate on it.

To think that one is the body is ignorance.

God is sat and everything else is asat—to know this is knowledge.

Happiness and sorrow, birth and death, disease and grief—all these exist so long as one has the idea that 'I am this body'. These belong to the body, not to atman...after one attains knowledge of the Self, one sees happiness and suffering, and birth and death as dream-like.

GOD WITH AND WITHOUT FORM

The same being who has taken form is also formless. To the devotee He appears with form. Think of a great ocean—water and water on all sides, but at some places, water has solidified into ice because of the cold. Just like that, one sees God with form on account of devotion. The same ice melts when the sun rises. Similarly, when the sun of knowledge rises, the form melts into the formless.

It is enough to have faith in one path. If you believe in formless God, that is good. However, do not think that this alone is true and all else is false. Know that formless God is true and God with form is also true.

God is not merely formless; God assumes form as well. One can see godly forms in meditative states of mind, with a heart full for devotion. The Divine Mother appears before us in many forms.

If you ask which form of God to contemplate upon—meditate on any form that you like. But know that all represent the same God.

BRAHMAN

What Brahman is cannot be described in words. Everything else has been defiled by speech. Veda, Purana, Tantra, the six schools of philosophy—all have been defiled by utterance. But there is only one thing which has not been thus defiled, and that is Brahman. What Brahman is, nobody has been able to put in words.

Brahman, which is sat, is eternal—existent at all times, past, present, and future—and is without beginning and end. Brahman cannot be described in words. At most one can say—He is consciousness itself, bliss itself.

Brahman is unattached. One can find a pleasant smell or a foul smell in the air, but the air itself is without such qualities.

Brahman is like infinite space.
Brahman is unchangeable—just like fire
that has no colour.

SHAKTI[37]

Whom the Vedas call Brahman, I call the same being Mother. That being who is without finite attributes is also with attributes; that which is Brahman is also shakti. When seen as non-active, we call it Brahman. When we think it is involved in the process of creation, preservation, and destruction, we call Her Adyashakti,[38] Kali.

The One who is sat is called Brahman, another name is kala[39] (mahakala).... 'Kali' or

[37]Power; in this context, refers to the Divine Feminine.
[38]Primal energy.
[39]Time.

Adyashakti is the one who is in union with kala.
Kala and Kali—
Brahman and shakti—are abheda.[40]

Brahman and its shakti are abheda. When non-active, we call it brahman; when engaged in the threefold action of creation, preservation, and destruction, we call it shakti. But it is the same entity. When you say 'fire', it automatically indicates its power to burn; when you think of the power to burn, you are reminded of fire. You cannot think of one without thinking of the other.

Chitshakti (Adyashakti) and the Brahman of Vedanta are abheda. Like water and its power to make ice.... Like snake and its slithering

[40]Not different; the word is part of the Indian philosophical terminology and is usually translated as 'non-different'.

movement. When do we call it Brahman? When it is non-active or uninvolved. When a man wears clothes, he remains the same man.... The snake has poison, but it is nothing to the snake; it is poison for those whom the snake will bite. Brahman is thus uninvolved. Wherever there is name and form, it is the play of prakriti[41].... All this is the play of Chitshakti—even meditation and the one who meditates. So long as you have this feeling that you are meditating, you are in Her domain.

One cannot have the vision of God unless Mahamaya[42] makes way. One needs the grace

[41]The feminine principle.

[42]Another name of the Divine Feminine or Adyashakti. The idea is that the ensnaring phenomenal world is sustained and perpetuated by Her; this is Her divine play. However, if one is yearning for true knowledge and liberation, then the grace of Mahamaya can help destroy one's ignorance and worldly attachment.

of Mahamaya. That is why we worship shakti.

All women are the representation of shakti. It is Adyashakti who has taken the female form.

MOTHERHOOD OF GOD

The same Supreme Being is called 'Mother'. Mother is the source of great love. God can be attained through love.

I had worshipped my own mother with flowers and sandalwood. The Divine Mother has taken the form of our mothers.

Matribhava[43] is the last word of sadhana. 'You are Mother, and I am your son'—this is the last word.

Matribhava is a pure attitude.

[43]Motherly attitude.

GOD IN THE WORLD

God is present in all beings as the all-pervading entity. He is present even in the ant. But there is a difference in the degree of manifestation.

Take, for example, the bel[44] fruit. Someone separated the shell, the seeds, and the flesh. Then somebody wanted to know the weight of the bel. Now, can you find out the weight of the bel by weighing the flesh alone? You have to weigh the shell, seeds, and the flesh all together. Initially you had reasoned that neither shell nor seeds, but the flesh is the

[44]Scientific name: Aegle marmelos.

real thing. Now you have to reason that the shell and the seeds belong to the same thing to which the flesh belongs. Similarly, you first reason 'neti', 'neti'—'not this', 'not this'. Not this world, nor its creatures, Brahman alone is of substance, and the rest is not of any essence. Later you realize that the world and its living beings have originated in the same Brahman.

Someone: If one's mind goes to God how can one continue to live in the household?

Sri Ramakrishna: What? If you would no longer stay in the household, where would you go? I see that wherever I stay, I stay in Rama's Ayodhya. This whole world is Rama's Ayodhya. After attaining knowledge from his guru, Rama said he would renounce the world.... Vasishtha asked, 'Rama, first reason with me, then you give up the world. Tell me, is the world devoid of God? If that is so, you may renounce [it].' Rama realized that God has verily become the world and all the creatures.

God has become this world; He has become the twenty-four cosmic principles.[45]

God resides not merely within all. God resides within and without! In the Kali temple, the Divine Mother showed me that everything is imbued with divine consciousness. Mother has become all! Idol, me, utensils, threshold, marble floor—everything is full of pure consciousness.

---

[45]According to Samkhya philosophy there are twenty-four cosmic principles or evolutes of nature: prakriti, mahat, ahamkara, manas, the five sense organs, five organs of action, five tanmatras, and five mahabhutas.

God is within and without... That is why the Vedas say 'tat tvam asi'.[46] It is on account of maya that we see the world as manifold, but essentially it is God.

[46]'You are that', Upanishadic saying denoting the advaitic position of non-duality.

GOD IN MAN

When I see a swarm of human beings, my mind is kindled with the thought of God.

When our hands and feet move, people say the body is moving! They do not know it is God who resides within who is moving. They say the hand got burnt in water!
Water cannot burn anything. The hand got burnt by the heat that is in hot water. Rice is cooking in the pot. The vegetables are jumping inside. A child thinks the vegetables are dancing on their own! He doesn't know there is fire beneath! Similarly, human beings think the sense organs work on their own. They are not aware—it is pure

consciousness that is within
that makes things work.

It is said that human beings are greater than even the shaligram.[47] We say 'naranarayana'.[48] If one has that kind of intense bhakti, then one has the vision of God in man himself.

---

[47]A stone naturally containing auspicious marks of Vishnu, considered particularly holy and worshipped as a special manifestation of Narayana.

[48]Narayana or Vishnu manifest in nara, that is, man.

SERVICE OF GOD IN MAN

Compassion for all beings? Who are you to have compassion for all beings? No, no, not compassion—but Shiva jnane jiva seva, serving man knowing him to be God.

ADVAITA[49]

Unless one has advaitajnana, that is, unless one realizes that there is but one reality, one cannot have the vision of pure consciousness.

First tie the knot of advaita in the corner of your cloth, then do as you please.

[49]Non-duality, non-dual consciousness.

RELIGIOUS DIVERSITY & HARMONY

God can be attained by different paths. For example, some of you have come here in a carriage, some by boat, some by steamer, some others by foot, whatever was convenient for each of you, and whatever was suitable as per your nature. The destination is the same—some have arrived earlier, some later.

We call the same God by many names. Like the Hindus call water 'jal', the Christians call it 'water', Muslims call it 'pani', and so on.

One should never think that one's own religion alone is true, and others are false.

God can be attained through all paths. One only needs to have sincere yearning. There exist infinite number of paths, and infinite number of ideas about God.

If one is sincere, one can attain God with the help of any religion. The Vaishnavas will also attain God, the Shaktas too, the Vedantins too, the Brahmos too; and Muslims and Christians—all of them will reach God. All sincere seekers will find God.

I practised every religion once—Hinduism, Islam, Christianity, even Shakta, Vaishnava, Vedantic—I had to walk all these paths. I saw that everybody comes to the same God by different paths.

The one who has been able to harmonize is a sensible human being. Most people are

monotonous. But I see that all represent the same reality. Shakta, Vaishnava, Vedantic—all doctrines talk about the same God. The One who is formless is also with form, and also assumes different forms.... The One whom the Vedas describe is also the One whom Tantra or the Puranas describe. The one and only Sacchidananda...the Vedas say 'Om Sachhidananda Brahma'; Tantra says 'Om Sachhidananda Shiva'...; Puranas say 'Om Sachhidananda Krishna'. The same Sachhidananda is described in the Vedas, Puranas, and Tantra. And the scriptures of the Vaishnavas also say—
Krishna had become Kali.

HOW TO FIND GOD

What good is it to only realize that God exists? The vision of God is not the last word. One needs to bring Him home, and converse with Him. Some have heard about milk, some have seen milk, and some have drunk it. Some people have seen the king. But only a few can bring him home and treat him to a meal.

Someone: How to focus one's mind on God?
Sri Ramakrishna: Always chant the name of God. And keep company with holy people—sadhus and God's devotees—one should seek them out. If you are in the midst of worldly work day and night, it is not easy to keep

one's mind on God. It is very necessary to live in seclusion at times and think of God. In the initial stages of sadhana, it is very difficult to keep one's mind focused on God unless one lives in seclusion occasionally. When you plant a sapling, you have to fence it in order to protect it.

When three kinds of attraction come together, one has the vision of God—the attraction a worldly person feels for objects of enjoyment, that which a mother feels for her child, and that which a devoted wife feels for her husband. If someone experiences these three kinds of attraction together for God, by virtue of that love alone he can attain God. The point is, one has to love God just like a mother loves her child, a devoted wife loves her husband, and a worldly person loves objects of enjoyment.

One has to call upon God with intense yearning. A kitten only knows how to call its mother with 'mew, mew'. It stays where its mother keeps it—sometimes in the kitchen, at times on the floor, again at times on the bed. When it is in pain, it only utters 'mew, mew', it doesn't know anything else. Wherever its mother is, she comes after hearing its call.

Unless one yearns for God, one does not have His vision. This yearning does not come unless one has reached the end of enjoyment. Those who are immersed in worldly enjoyment do not experience this yearning for God.

If one cries with intense yearning for God, one has His vision. People cry for wife and children, they cry profusely for wealth, but who weeps for God? One has to call upon God sincerely.

Yearning! Just as a child cries helplessly for his mother when he cannot see her, if one cries for God with such yearning, one can even attain God by that.

One needs to reflect and discriminate constantly. What is there in wealth, and what is there in a beautiful body? Reflect! Even in the body of a beautiful woman, there are but bones, flesh, fat, and excrement. Why are human beings attracted to these things, leaving aside God? Why do human beings forget God?

Take a deep plunge. Learn to love God. Be immersed in love for God.

Someone: Can one see God?

Sri Ramakrishna: Yes, of course, God can be seen. Occasionally living in seclusion, recounting the glories of God, reflecting and discriminating between the everlasting and the ephemeral—by these methods can one attain God.

Scriptures and books—of what use are they? Unless you have obtained God's grace, nothing is of help. Strive earnestly so that you may acquire His grace. When you have His grace, you will have His vision. He will talk to you.

Someone: Sir, can one find God while leading a householder's life?

Sri Ramakrishna: Definitely one can. But as I said, keeping holy company and constant prayer are essential. One needs to weep before God. When the impurities of one's mind are thus washed away, then one has His vision. The mind is like an iron needle sullied with mud, and God is like a magnet. Unless the mud is removed, the needle does not come in contact with the magnet. Tears wash away the mud. This mud is desire, anger, greed, sinfulness, worldliness. The moment the mud is washed away, the magnet will attract the needle—that is, one will have the vision of God. One attains Him after one's heart is purified.

The mind has got dispersed—part of it has gone to Dhaka, part to Delhi, and another part to Cooch Behar. You need to gather the mind at one point. If you want cloth worth sixteen annas, you have to pay the seller sixteen annas. If there is even a little disturbance, there won't be union with God. If there is a hole in the telegraph wire, you won't be able to transmit the message.

Abhyasayoga![50] One has to practise calling upon God every day. It doesn't happen in one day. When you call upon God every day, in due course you develop longing for Him.

Give up attachment to worldly objects through abhyasayoga. The Gita says the same thing. Through practise, the mind acquires exceptional powers. Then it becomes much easier to control the workings of one's senses, and vices such as desire, anger, and so on.

[50]The habitual practise of something.

One needs to undertake intense sadhana for God-realization.

BHAKTI–LOVE FOR GOD

The jnani reasons 'neti', 'neti' and renounces the world as unreal.... That is one path. The path of jnana-bhakti is also a path. Bhakti is another path. Jnana yoga is true, and so is the path of bhakti—one can reach God through different paths. Till the time He keeps one's ego, the path of bhakti is easier.

When one has bhakti,
nothing else is required.

One who has no spiritual know-how, but has loving devotion for God and has the desire to know Him—such a person can attain God just by the dint of such devotion.

God surrenders easily to loving devotion.

But ordinary bhakti is not enough. Without premabhakti[51] one does not attain God. Another name for premabhakti is ragabhakti. Unless one develops love for God, one does not have God-realization.

One does not experience premabhakti unless one has an intense love for God. And along with it the feeling that 'God is my own'. Once, three friends were passing through a forest when they came across a tiger. One of them said, 'Brother! We are all dead now!' Another said, 'How can we die! Come, let us call upon God!' The third one said, 'Why trouble God? Come, let us climb this tree.'

[51]Devotion imbued with ecstatic love for the Divine.

The man who said 'We are all dead now' does not know that God is the protector. The one who said 'Let us call upon God' knows that it is God who governs the process of creation, preservation, and destruction. And the one who said 'Why trouble God?' is the one who has developed love for God. The nature of love is that it considers the beloved as somebody who needs care and protection. Why bother the beloved! The only desire of the one who loves is that not even a thorn should prick the feet of the beloved!

There is another kind of bhakti. It is called vaidhi bhakti.[52] One has to do so many counts of japa,[53] one has to fast, go on pilgrimage,

[52]Rule-bound devotion.

[53]Repetition of God's name or mantra given at the time of spiritual initiation.

perform ritualistic worship with so many offerings, perform many sacrifices—all this is vaidhi bhakti. For most people, after doing all this, perhaps someday they acquire ragabhakti. But unless one has ragabhakti one does not attain God. One has to love God. Worldliness will disappear completely and only the thought of God will occupy one's mind—it is only then that one will attain God.

Everybody does not experience prema.[54] Gouranga[55] did. Ordinary human beings can experience up to divine ecstasy. Incarnations and isvarakotis[56] experience prema. When one

[54]A particularly pure and exalted form of love, bordering on ecstasy.
[55]Sri Chaitanya. He had spells of divine ecstasy, in which he lost all sense of the outer world and sang and danced and wept in ecstatic love for God. He is also known as an epitome of compassion for suffering humanity.
[56]Highly evolved souls who are specially deputed to take human birth to aid God's work in the world.

experiences prema, the entire world appears non-existent, even one's own body— which is such an object of love for all— even that body seems unreal.

You do not want anything from God, but you love Him just like that—this is called ahetuki bhakti,[57] shuddha bhakti.[58] Prahlad[59] had this; he did not want kingdom or wealth, he only wanted Hari.

Love for God is like a rope. God is bound by such love.

[57]Bhakti without any motive or expectation.

[58]Pure bhakti.

[59]The great devotee of Vishnu; he accepted the tortures of his father, asura king, Hiranyakashipu, for the sake of his devotion to God. In order to save him and kill Hiranyakashipu, Vishnu incarnated as Narasimha (half-lion, half-man form).

Just like a devotee of God cannot live without God, similarly God cannot live without His devotee.

God is present in His devotee in a special way. A devotee is God's living room or parlour.

THREE ATTITUDES TOWARDS GOD

Hanuman said, 'O Rama, at times I think you are the whole, and I am part; at times I think you are the master and I am your servant. Again, when I have knowledge, I see that you are me and I am you'.

RENUNCIATION

The fruit of reading the Gita is that which happens when one utters the word 'Gita' ten times—gita, gi ta gi tagi,[60] tagi, tagi.... What does it mean? Listen ye!
Renounce everything and take refuge at the feet of the Lord!

God cannot be attained without renunciation.

Complete renunciation is not for the householder. The householder will renounce in his mind. But a sannyasin is to renounce completely—internally as well as externally.

[60]Corrupt form of the word 'tyagi', meaning 'one who has renounced'.

Renounce in your mind...if you can live in this world without attachment and seek God with sincerity, you will attain God-realization.

If by God's grace one develops intense renunciation, one can be saved from attachment to objects of worldly desire. Do you know what is intense renunciation? 'We'll attain God someday, let's wait till then'—this is an inferior form of renunciation. The one who experiences intense renunciation, his heart yearns for God, just like a mother's heart longs for her son. The one who has intense renunciation does not want anything other than God.... 'First let me take care of my family, then I'll think of God'—he doesn't think like that at all.

There is a great deal of difference between a devotee who renounces everything for God and a devotee who is still ensnared in worldly attachment. The one who renounces everything is like a bee. A bee does not sit on anything except flowers. It does not drink anything but honey. Worldly-minded devotees are like flies—at times they sit on sweetmeat, and at times on a rotten wound. They think about God, but at times they are attracted to worldly enjoyment. The one with the spirit of renunciation is like the pied cuckoo. The pied cuckoo does not drink any water other than water from the monsoon clouds caused by the Swati constellation. Seven oceans and rivers are all full of water, yet it will not drink water from any other source!

GOD'S NAME

Earlier, when people had fever, they got cured with elaborately prepared remedies. But now when we have malarial fever, we need D. Gooptu's[61] mixture. Earlier, people used to perform yajnas,[62] and practise severe austerities for God-realization. But now, in this age, people's lives are driven by hunger, and the mind is weak—if one utters God's name mindfully that alone can destroy the disease of worldliness.

---

[61]Dr Dwarakanath Gooptu (1818–82), who patented a medicine for malarial fever.

[62]Vedic rituals.

Taking God's name purifies one's body and mind.

If one can have an attraction for and faith in the name of God, one does not need any other kind of sadhana. Under the influence of God's name, all doubts disappear, the mind is purified, and one eventually attains Sacchidananda.

One attains devotion by constantly repeating God's name.

Those who do not know anything other than God take God's name with every breath.... One should keep constant remembrance of God.

When you see tears roll at the name of God and one experiences spiritual ecstasy, know for sure that worldly desires have disappeared and one has attained God.

God's name and God are not different—knowing this, one is to always chant the name of God with love.

IDOLS

You were talking about worship of the earthen idol. Even if it is a clay image, there is value in such worship. Different forms of worship have been instituted by God Himself. The One to whom this world belongs has arranged for all these, depending on the different needs of different individuals. A mother arranges for different kinds of food depending on the capacity of each of her children.

A certain mother has five sons. She is to cook fish today. She is making different fish dishes! For one son, she is making fish poloa, for one, fish ambal, for another, fish chacchari, for another fried fish—she is making different preparations. Each will eat according to his liking and according to what suits his stomach.

We are reminded of our father when we see his photograph. Just like that, by worshipping the idol of God, in due course one gets a glimpse of God.

RITUALS

Ritualistic worship, yajna, and so on are nothing. Once one develops love for God, then one no longer needs these things. Until there is wind, one needs a fan; but when the southern breeze blows, one can put away the fan.

PILGRIMAGE

There are two kinds of sadhu—bahudak and kutichak. The kind who still roams about in pilgrimage, whose mind has not yet attained peace is called bahudak. But the one who is done with pilgrimages, whose mind is content—he settles in one place.

It is true, however, that one is easily reminded of God in a place of pilgrimage.

SCRIPTURE

Can one find God with the help of scriptures? After reading scriptures, at most one has the idea that God exists. But unless we dive deep, God does not appear before us. When God reveals Himself on his own, then all doubts disappear. No matter how much you read or how much you quote from the scriptures, unless you have intense longing for God, you won't get hold of Him. People can be impressed by erudition, but one can't impress God with that.

One needs to know the essence of the scriptures from the guru's mouth. And then engage in sadhana. Somebody wrote a letter...the letter asked to send five kilos of sweetmeat and one saree. After reading, one threw away the letter and started arranging for the sweetmeat and the saree. Similarly, once you know the essence of the scriptures, what's the point in continuing reading? Now it's time for sadhana.

What is the use of mere erudition? A scholar may know many a Sanskrit verse or many scriptures but one whose mind is attracted to objects of worldly enjoyment will not be able to assimilate the essence of the scriptures—his reading of the scriptures is in vain. It's written in the almanac—there'll be so much rainfall; but if you squeeze the almanac—not a single drop will fall.

One does not understand the meaning of scriptures unless one has done sadhana. What is the point in uttering 'siddhi' 'siddhi'?[63] ...Even applying siddhi all over one's body doesn't make one intoxicated. One has to drink siddhi for intoxication.

Scriptures have two kinds of meaning—the meaning of the words and the essence of the message. One needs to accept the essential meaning—that which matches with direct revelation from God. There is a great deal of difference between what is written in a letter and what the writer himself says. Scriptures are like the written letter; revelation from God is hearing things directly from God's mouth. I do not accept anything unless I verify it directly with the Divine Mother.

The Gita is the essence of all scriptures.

---

[63]An intoxicating drink.

SURRENDER

Can you know God through reasoning? Call upon Him after surrendering yourself and taking refuge in Him.

Give God the power of attorney! If a good person is entrusted with a responsibility, will that person do anything wrong? Entrust God with all responsibility and be carefree.

Those whom God Himself is holding have no fear. The boy who holds his father while walking on an incline in a field might fall if he absent-mindedly lets go of his father's hand. But when the father himself holds the son, he cannot fall.

SADHANA

True sadhana is to follow one's word. Otherwise, one says 'Oh God, You are my all in all', but thinks of the material world as all in one's mind—such a person's sadhana is futile.

Meditate in the depths of your mind, in a corner, and in the forest. And always discriminate between sat and asat. God alone is sat—eternal, and everything else is asat—ephemeral. Discriminating thus, renounce the ephemeral in your mind.

In order to attain devotion for God one needs to spend time in seclusion. If you want to obtain butter, you have to let the milk sit undisturbed. If one disturbs it, one will have no curd. Thereafter one has to sit in the quiet, leaving all other work aside, and churn the curd to obtain butter.

With the help of your mind if you contemplate on God in seclusion, you attain knowledge, non-attachment, and devotion. But if you leave the same mind in the midst of worldly affairs, it becomes base.

This world is like water, and the mind is like milk. If you leave milk in the water, it gets mixed; you can no longer separate pure milk. But if you obtain curd from milk, then churn butter out of it, and leave that butter in water, it floats.

That is why one is to first obtain the butter

that is knowledge and devotion by doing sadhana in seclusion.

The rishis[64] of yore attained the knowledge of Brahman. If one has even the slightest trace of worldliness, one cannot acquire the knowledge of Brahman. How hard the rishis used to work! They used to leave their ashrams early in the morning; then they spent the entire day alone, absorbed in meditation. After returning to their ashrams at night, they partook of some fruits at most. Seeing, hearing, touching—they used to keep their minds away from such things. That's how they could have a direct perception of Brahman.

[64]A seer; literally, one who could see or apprehend the divine mantras.

GURU

God Himself is guru.

If the guru is not competent, then it is woe for both guru and disciple. The ego of the disciple persists and, along with it, his worldly bondages. The disciple does not attain liberation if his guru is not competent.

Not everybody can be a guru. Huge logs remain afloat in water, and many birds and animals can also cross the river aboard these. But if a creature sits atop a log that is good for nothing, the log sinks, taking with it the creature that is atop it. That is why in every age, for the sake of guiding humankind, God Himself takes human birth as guru.

Everybody will attain liberation. But one has to follow the instructions of one's guru. If one takes the winding path, it will be difficult to find one's way. Liberation will come after much delay. Perhaps it won't come even in this birth, but after many more births.

Faith in the words of the guru! If one proceeds following his words, one attains God.

HOLY COMPANY

Sri Ramakrishna: God and His riches! This world represents His riches. But everybody gets swayed by His riches, they do not look for Him to whom it all belongs.

A devotee: What is the way out?

Sri Ramakrishna: The way out is holy company and prayer.

Unless you go to the physician, your disease will not be cured. It is not enough to be in the company of holy men once, their company is needed all the time; the disease is persistent. The other way is earnest prayer. He is your very own, tell Him, you want to see how He is—He has to come!

Someone: What is the benefit of holy company?

Sri Ramakrishna: You develop love for God. Unless you have real yearning, nothing happens. As a result of continuous holy company, your heart will crave for God. Just like when somebody in the family is sick, the mind is all the time restless as to how the disease will be cured. Again, if somebody loses a job, he roams from office to office looking for a job, restless—one needs to develop a similar restlessness for God.

When we see a lawyer, we are reminded of the court and legal cases; when we see doctors, we are reminded of disease and medicine. Similarly, when we see sadhus and devotees, we are reminded of God.

NON-ATTACHMENT

Let the boat be in water, but not water inside the boat, else you will drown. A spiritual seeker can live in this world, but worldliness should not inhabit his mind.

If you take a dive in deep waters, you might be attacked by a crocodile. But if you have applied turmeric paste before diving, the crocodile will not touch you. In the deep waters of the human heart, there are six crocodiles, namely lust, anger, greed, attachment, pride, and envy. But if you apply the turmeric of viveka[65] and vairagya,[66] these crocodiles will stay away.

[65]The discrimination between the eternal and the ephemeral.
[66]Dispassion.

WORLDLY PEOPLE

Worldly people get bound in this world because of their desires; their hands and feet get tied. And they think that all happiness lies in this pursuit of worldly pleasure.... They don't know that it is this very thing that brings upon death. When worldly people die, their wives weep, saying 'You left us like this! What will happen to me!' But so great is their worldly attachment that the very next moment, when they see the lamp burning too bright, they say 'Lower the wick, it's using too much oil.' While death is standing just round the corner!

Worldly people do not think about God. If they find time, they either talk nonsense, or do foolish work. If asked, they say, 'I can't sit quietly, that is why I am making a fence!' They play cards when they feel bored.

Worldly people have another tendency. If you take them away from their worldly life and keep them in a blissful place, they will die of boredom. The worm that feeds on feces is happy when it is on feces; if you keep it in the rice pot, it will die!

THE HUMAN MIND

The human mind is like a sack of mustard seeds. When the seeds get dispersed, it is difficult to gather them again. Similarly, once a person's mind gets dispersed in the maze of worldliness, it is very difficult to recollect it and make it composed again.

It is all a matter of the mind. One is bound in the mind and free in the mind.
The colour in which you dye your mind, the mind takes on that colour... It is all in the mind.... So, liberate your mind!

'I am a free soul, whether I stay in the household or in the forest, what bondage do I have? I am God's child, the son of the king of kings, who can bind me?'.... 'I am not bound, I am free'—if one says this to oneself forcefully, it comes true. One becomes free.

One can see God. The Vedas say He is beyond the apprehension of speech and mind—this essentially means He is beyond the reach of the worldly mind.... God can be known through the pure mind, pure intelligence. That is why keeping holy company, praying, following the guru's instructions—all these are necessary. They purify the mind. Once the mind is purified, one has the vision of God. Dirty water is cleaned only when you put alum in it. Then you can see your face reflected in it. One can't see one's face in a dirty mirror.

When the mind becomes free from attachment, one has the vision of God. Whatever comes into the pure mind, that is His voice. Pure mind, pure intelligence, pure atman—are all one and the same thing. There is nothing except God that is pure.

Till the time you reason with your mind, you cannot reach the Absolute. When you reason with your mind, you cannot leave aside the phenomenal world, you cannot avoid the action of the senses—form, taste, smell, touch, sound. One attains knowledge of Brahman when all reasoning stops. One cannot know the atman with *this* mind. It is only through the atman that the atman can be known. The pure mind, pure intelligence, and pure atman—these are all one and the same thing.

As long as this finite mind is working, how will you say that the world does not exist or you do not exist? When this mind is annihilated, and with it all thought-waves subside, then samadhi happens—knowledge of Brahman dawns. But, sa re ga ma pa dha ni—one cannot stay on the note ni for long.

The mind is expended uselessly when it is used for worldly work. Eventually it is harmful for the mind.

ADVICE TO HOUSEHOLDERS

That you have entered into householder's life—what harm is there in it? It is even easier to do sadhana there—just like fighting a battle from inside a fort.... One just needs to keep one's family satisfied, one needs to look after their upkeep. Then it is much easier to undertake sadhana.

In the world, one has to battle against desire, anger, and such other vices, one has to battle against attachment. It is better if this battle takes place from within a fort. It is better to fight from the safety of one's home—one gets food for sustenance, if one's wife is virtuous, she helps in different ways...instead of roaming about in ten places looking for food, it is better to obtain it from one place. It is like fighting a battle from inside a fort.

I say solemnly that there is no harm that you have entered the householder's life. But you have to keep your minds fixed on God. Otherwise, you can't attain God. Perform your duties with one hand, and with the other hand hold on to to God. When you are done with your household life, hold on to God with both hands.

Do all your work, but offer your mind to God. Wife, son, father, mother—stay with them and serve them all. As if they are your own. But in your heart, know that they are nobody to you. The maid-servant in the house of the rich man does all the work, but her mind lies with her own home in the village. She even brings up their children as her own, and calls them 'my Ram', 'my Hari'. But she knows in the heart of her hearts that they are nobody to her.

The tortoise spends the day in water, but do you know where lies its mind? On the shore, where it has kept its eggs. Do all your work, but keep your mind immersed in the thought of God.

If you get involved in the world without having attained devotion to God, you will get more and more attached. You will easily get impatient with trouble, grief and suffering. The more you think of worldly objects, the more attached you will become.

Before plucking the jackfruit, one is to apply oil on one's hands. Otherwise, one's hands get smeared with gum. Similarly, one is to lay one's hands on worldly work after obtaining the oil that is devotion to God.

If a householder is a true devotee of God, he performs his work with non-attachment. He surrenders the fruits of his action—gain, loss, happiness, grief—all to God. And day and night he prays to God for devotion, he wants nothing else. This is called nishkam karma[67]—work without attachment.

Live in this world like an ant. In this world, the real and the unreal are mixed up—like sand and sugar mixed up. Be like an ant and get hold of only the sugar. Milk and

[67]Work done without any expectation of reward or benefit.

water are all mixed up—the bliss of pure consciousness and the pleasures of the world are all mixed up. Like a swan, reject the water and partake of only the milk.

Live in this world like a leftover leaf plate blown away by the wind. At times, the wind takes the plate inside the house, at times on to the dump. The plate moves in the direction in which the wind moves, at times to a good place, at times to a bad place!

After attaining God-realization, one can live in the world without attachment. I have seen village women—when a village woman pounds rice, with one hand she moves the grain, with another she breastfeeds her child, and at the same time she talks to a customer—'You owe me two anna—remember to pay it.' But three-fourths of her attention is on her hand—lest the pestle falls on it! Similarly, keeping three-fourths of one's mind focused on God, with the remaining do your work!

VIJNANA

Go beyond jnana[68] and ajnana;[69] only then you will come to know God. To know this universe as manifold is ajnana. The egotism of erudition is also ajnana. One and only God is present in all beings—this knowledge is called jnana. To know Him in a special or more intimate way is called vijnana. For instance, a thorn has pierced your foot; in order to pluck that thorn, you need another thorn. Once the first thorn is removed, you throw away both the thorns. In order to remove the thorn of ajnana, you need to obtain the thorn of jnana.

---

[68]Knowledge.
[69]Ignorance.

Then you need to throw away both jnana and ajnana. God is beyond both jnana and ajnana.

To know this world as manifold is ajnana. To know it as one is jnana—that is, one and only God is present in all beings. To have a direct conversation with Him is called vijnana—to attain God and then love Him in various ways is called vijnana.

Vijnana is knowing God in a more intimate way. There is fire in wood—this knowledge is called jnana. To cook rice in that fire, to eat that rice, and obtain nutrition from it—this is called vijnana. To know that God exists is called jnana. To converse with Him, to enjoy Him by adopting a particular attitude—vatsalya, sakhya, dasya, madhura—

this is called vijnana. God has become this world—to realize this is vijnana.

The vijnani sees that the same Brahman, who is beyond the three gunas,[70] is also Bhagavan[71] possessing the six great qualities.[72]

[70]According to Samkhya philosophy, the material world is comprised of three gunas or qualities—sattva (equilibrium, light), rajas (activity, pride), and tamas (inertia, darkness).
[71]Another name used in Hinduism to denote God with attributes.
[72]Bhagavan is one who possesses bhaga or the six great qualities: knowledge, possessions, power, strength, courage, and splendour.

AFTER GOD-REALIZATION

A salt doll went to measure the ocean. As soon as it stepped in, it dissolved! Who will measure the ocean now? The one who went to measure exists no more! The mind is annihilated in the seventh plane of consciousness,[73] and a person enters into samadhi. What one experiences in samadhi cannot be put in words.

Kacha[74] was immersed in nirvikalpa samadhi.[75] When his mind came down from

---

[73]The human mind has seven planes of consciousness: the base, sex organs, navel, heart, throat, the region between the eyebrows, and the crown of the head.

[74]Son of the sage Brihaspati.

[75]The highest state of samadhi where thoughts subside completely and one has a vision of the Absolute.

that elevated state, somebody asked him, 'What do you see now?' Kacha replied, 'I see that the world is, as if, soaked in God. Everything is filled with God. He has become all that I see.'

What is the state of a paramahamsa? If you give a swan milk mixed with water, it will drink the milk and leave behind the water. Just like that, a paramahamsa partakes of that which is of essence in this world, that is, God, and gives up that which is inessential.

A paramahamsa is like a child—he has no sense of who is his kin and who is a stranger, no bondage of worldly relationships.... Like a child, he has no calculation as to what he is doing. He sees everything as filled with divine consciousness.

After complete God-realization, one's nature becomes like that of a five-year-old child—one then loses the sense of distinction between man and woman.

The one who has attained God becomes like a dry coconut (the shell and the flesh are separated)—the sense that 'I am this body' disappears completely. He no longer feels that the pleasure and pain of the body are his pleasure and pain.
He no longer seeks comfort for his body.
He roams about as a jivanmukta.

The one who has attained God-realization, has merely the trace of desire, anger, and so on. Just like a burnt rope. Only the form of the rope exists. But the moment you blow it, it dissipates.

So long as there are paddy seeds, they'll grow into rice plants when sown. But if you boil the paddy and then sow them, they will no longer grow into plants. Similarly, those who have attained God, they are no longer bound to be born again in this world.

VARIA

God smiles twice. Once, when brothers measure and divide land between themselves, saying 'This side is mine, that side is yours.' He smiles again when a man is critically ill, his relatives are weeping, and the physician comes and assures them, 'Don't worry. I'll cure him.' The doctor doesn't know—if God decides to put an end to the man's life, who can save him!

Some people think that contemplating too much on God makes one lose one's mind. It is not at all so! This is a pool of nectar, an ocean of ambrosia! The Vedas have called

Him 'amrita',[76] one does not die if one gets drowned in it—on the contrary, one becomes immortal.

Does one lose one's consciousness by contemplating on pure consciousness? Does one lose one's sanity by thinking about God? God is pure intelligence.

The water of Ganga is not ordinary water, the dust of Vrindavan is not ordinary dust, and the mahaprasad of Sri Sri Jagannath is not ordinary rice. These three represent Brahman.

---

[76]Nectar, ambrosia; that which makes one immortal.